ENTREPRENEURIAL 101

How to start your
own business
and avoid
costly mistakes

Doug Wells

Entrepreneurial 101

www.wells2000.com

Because of the dynamic nature of the Internet, any Web addresses or links contained in this book may have changed since publication and may no longer be valid.

ISBN-10:   0-9837065-5-7
ISBN-13:   978-0-9837065-5-7

Thinking of starting a business?

This book will help

you gain valuable information

and *avoid costly mistakes*.

It is estimated that 50% of businesses fail within the first year and more than 75% to 85% of new businesses do not make their fifth year anniversary. This amount can only be estimated since a lot of new businesses are created every minute but do not ever get counted by any governmental agency. This book contains the basic building blocks for starting a business. This book is designed to provide you with the information you will need to start your own business, and added information to continue being successful.

This book will give you an overview of the following:

- THE ENTREPRENEURIAL PERSONALITY
- PROS AND CONS OF SELF-EMPLOYMENT
- THE BUSINESS IDEA
- RESEARCH THE IDEA
- WRITING THE BUSINESS PLAN
- FINANCES
- KEEPING RECORDS
- GETTING STARTED
- TAXES
- MARKETING
- PROFESSIONALISM
- OWNERS CHECKLIST
- SUMMING IT UP
- HELPFUL RESOURCES

THE ENTREPRENEURIAL PERSONALITY

There are certain qualities which distinguish entrepreneurs from the rest of the pack.

High need for achievement
People who are content with their 9-to-5 job, on the average, do not prefer to be personally responsible for their self-assigned tasks.

Optimistic outlook
The willingness to take a chance (risk) and hope for the positive. In business, you must be willing to take a lot of chances and receive a lot of rejection, but view this as a stepping stone to your eventual success.

Self-motivation
This quality gets you going and keeps you moving. Being able to jump-start yourself over hurdles and obstacles regardless of the outcome, is a necessary trait for the entrepreneur.

Self-Confidence
Hand in hand with self-motivation, you must possess the confidence in yourself to portray to prospective clients that they will get the best their money can buy.

Decisiveness

The ability to operate independently and make the choice to succeed. To be successful you will need to make key decisions and stand behind them.

This is a small list of the traits most entrepreneurs have, but do not be discouraged if you are challenged in any one of these. It could mean starting a business by yourself is not a wise decision. However, that does not throw you out of the ownership market, it just gives you some parameters in choosing a partner to help in your endeavor. Take the following quiz and determine if you are ready to begin alone, or use the quiz in choosing a partner who compliments you in gaining the best foundation for your business.

THE QUIZ

Put a mark next to each statement which describes you. The statement does not have to be a perfect match to your personality, but it should be close.

- ❑ **Achievement**: I have the drive to achieve my ultimate potential for business success.
- ❑ **Cheerful:** I am generally a cheerful person and am happy talking with and interacting among others.
- ❑ **Competition:** I enjoy being competitive with others and look forward to the challenge.

- **Confidence:** I have the confidence in myself to be able to start and run a business.
- **Creativity:** I can address situations in innovative and imaginative ways to reach my goals.
- **Decisive:** I like to make decisions on my own, and am willing to take on the responsibility of them. I can make good sound judgments on difficult decisions.
- **Discipline:** I am self-motivated and can handle the necessary tasks which need completing, whether or not I like them.
- **Goal Orientated:** I know the importance of goal setting in my professional as well as personal life. I have the ability to follow through with goals I have set, which include long term goals as well as short term ones.
- **Health:** I have the physical and mental ability to solve problems and handle pressure without it taking a fatal direction.
- **Independent:** I am capable of working by myself, if necessary, and be responsible for my own actions.
- **Inquisitive:** I am willing to ask questions of others and seek out information needed.
- **Knowledge:** I have the necessary knowledge of myself and the products I wish to sell. I also understand that I do not know all there is, and will not hesitate to find out information needed.
- **Leadership:** I am able to direct people efficiently while still maintaining respect and compassion.

❑ **Motivation:** I have the motivation to overcome obstacles and continue with my goal to a prosperous business.

❑ **Networking:** I am able to draw from others the resources to support my business venture and utilize other businesses in the industry for the good of the industry as a whole.

❑ **Optimism:** I have a positive attitude and can set my mind to explore the potential of any situation.

❑ **Patience:** I have the patience and understanding that successful business do not happen overnight and time plus effort will equal a profitable venture.

❑ **Sociable:** I can walk up to people and start a conversation which likely will lead to sales. I am not phobic about talking with others and being in groups.

❑ **Trade Ability:** I am able to present to others information about my product and myself in an honest and persuasive way.

❑ **Work Ethic:** I am not afraid of hard work and do not procrastinate when something needs to be done.

Scoring

Add up all your tally marks. This is merely a tool to use in adding up your entrepreneurial profile points and determining for yourself where you fall short. The clues this quiz gives toward your success cannot be measured, but you should be able to examine and judge if a partner is needed.

14+: There is a good possibility you have the necessary qualities to be a successful business owner. It is possible you have worked in the past in managerial capacity for someone else and this will definitely aid you in achieving your goal of being a business owner.

7-13: You are essentially a positive person and should not have difficulty in operating a business. However, you will need to assess yourself on the certain traits which you have not marked, and continue to seek information to improve your chances of success.

0-6: The score is an indication you possibly should seek out a partner who has the missing traits and compliments you on your goals. This is an option worth considering at this time.

PROS AND CONS OF SELF-EMPLOYMENT

After you have assessed if you will be going at this alone or seeking out a complimentary partner, you need to understand there are pros as well as cons to owning your own business. Many people have the assumption owning a business is easy. You do not have to deal with an irate boss, can schedule in your own hours, take vacation when you want - the perfect job. Unfortunately this is not the case at all. Depending on the type of business you are interested in owning, and whether it will be part or full time, there are a lot of considerations to think about.

PROS

Being your own boss: having the authority and independence to make your own decisions.

Personal fulfillment, a sense of achievement and recognition.

The opportunity to make a living doing something you truly enjoy.

The ability to be creative, to design and develop your own idea, product or service.

Opportunity to build considerable wealth.

No limit to your earning potential.

No set schedule.

CONS

You accept multiple bosses and answer to them: government, customers, suppliers, etc.

The potential initial loss of spare time for personal and family life.

Administrative tasks are abundant and some time will be spent dealing with them.

High failure rates, fluctuating earnings.

Complete liability: if something goes wrong you can be held personally liable.

You are responsible for taxes.

No set schedule.

Not only are there pros and cons for starting a business, but there are also pros and cons for certain types of businesses, and how you enter the business (example: Home-based, new start-up Franchises, and Buying an existing business.). Do your homework well, find out as much information as you can about the type of business you want to start.

THE BUSINESS IDEA

You probably already have an idea for a business waiting in the wings, right? Usually people who want to start their own business have set on a specific idea and only want to own that type of business. A warning here: Some people start up a business because they see the opportunity of creating a great amount of money (in a short amount of time or not, it does not matter). The business you are about to start needs to be something **you enjoy doing**. Countless number of businesses have failed because the person who started it was only in the business for the money. Very few businesses have succeeded this way, so pick what you like. If being behind a desk is the worse place you can imagine, do not start up a business as a medical transcriptionist. When the obstacles come you will be more likely to give up before the race has even begun.

If you do what you LOVE, you will never WORK a day in your life.

If you have not decided on a business you can begin to narrow your choices. The following exercise will help you narrow down what may be a good business for you to be in. Before getting started have a copy of your recent resume. This exercise will give you a good idea of the skills you have obtained through hobbies, education, and jobs. It can be of great importance in determining what type of business is good for you. Look at the worksheet below. Notice the labels: *Education, Work Experience, Health Background, Other Experiences, Interests, Hobbies, Personal and Family Goals and*

Business Goals. Yes, this does resemble a job application or even your resume, however, this is not you trying to sell yourself. This is a realistic look at what you are capable, willing, and enjoy doing. This is only for you, and you will know when you're stretching it to make the business fit you.

> *I thought to myself, "I really like art and everyone is wearing t-shirts, many of these t-shirts have pictures on them. Maybe I can start a t-shirt business."*

Education:

Under Education list the courses you have taken which will be useful in your business (accounting, management, typing, law, etc.). In this area also include workshops, home courses, and mini seminars you have attended. Be as specific as possible about the amount of education you have obtained. Remember not all education is formal, anything you have learned should be placed here, even if it was a book you read.

Work Experience:

List not only the jobs you have held but the precise tasks which were required of you. Your work habits, and the traits you found helpful in holding these positions. Also list all the volunteer jobs you held, and whether or not you enjoyed them.

Health Background:

This is necessary if you have an illness, or reoccurring illness which might interfere with business. List allergies which could affect you (cleaning agents, perfumes, latex gloves, etc.). List restricted activities: back problems so minimal lifting.

Other Experiences:

This is the part most resumes will not have. Compile all the abilities you know how to do, even if you have never been to school or had to use them working for others; your green thumb, Internet capable, understand raising cows.

Interests:

What are you interested in? Put items such as working with children, reading, collecting things, being outside.

Hobbies:

List your hobbies. This area needs to be very full. A great deal of successful businesses have come from a hobby turned cash cow. Cooking, cleaning, finding bargains at the store.

Personal and Family Goals:

As well as your personal goals, list the goals you have for your family. Undoubtedly if you family goals and the business conflict, you are likely to fail, or worse off, lose your family. Place in here if your husband or wife will be supportive of the venture. Indicate six most important personal and family goals which you would like to accomplish in the next three years.

Business Goals:

Some personal and family goals will cross over into the business goals section (make enough money to live comfortably) but list them here too if they fall in the top six goals you want your business to accomplish. Although it is nice to dream about making a million dollars on your first sale, be realistic. This is not a guide for getting rich quick. It is to help secure you in having the basis for a successful business.

I don't really have any education in art or business. In fact I went to college to become a police officer, but I am sure there are classes or programs to learn the business side of a t-shirt shop. I worked at Pizza Hut going to college, so that won't help me much. I do know how to use computers pretty well. I am mechanically inclined. I have a pretty good idea of how to make a picture look cool. I can talk to people pretty good. I am healthy, strong and young. I enjoy sports and auto racing, a lot of them wear t-shirts with logos on them. I am sure I could get some of them to buy shirts from me. I would like to be able to spend time with my family while I earn money to support them. The business really just needs to pay my bills, I don't need to get rich. Although that would always be nice.

ASSESSING YOUR INTERESTS WORKSHEET

Education: _____

_____

_____

_____

Work Experience: _____

_____

_____

_____

Health Background: _____

_____

_____

Other Experiences: _____

_____

_____

_____

Interests: _____

_____

_____

_____

Hobbies: _____

_____

_____

_____

Personal and Family Goals: _____

_____

_____

_____

Business Goals: _____

_____

_____

_____

Now make a list of businesses you are interested in, and see which businesses you believe would match your qualifications. Write down a list of ten businesses which you believe you would like to start.

1. _____

_____

2. _____

_____

3. _____

_____

4. _____

_____

5. _____

_____

6. _____

_____

7. _____

_____

8. _____

_____

9. _____

_____

10. _____

_____

Begin to cross off ones which do not match your abilities. Yes you can always get educated to be able to run the business. If you are really interested in the business but do not have the qualifications, still keep the business on the list. Next to that business place what it would take to be knowledge in that business (a class at the local community college, a trade school, etc.). Consider all your likes and dislikes. Check out what your expectations of time and energy for this business are going to be. If you do not like to be up late, do not list an all-night copy store.

There are other resources for hundreds of ideas for businesses at the library, local college and universities, as well as the Internet. Even in most grocery stores there are magazines which list 100 businesses people are starting up. Once you have developed your list it is time to start the process of narrowing it down. Look over the list and be as critical as you can. Would you really enjoy owning a restaurant when it generally means being at work at 3 a.m.? In addition, the startup costs of owning even a small restaurant are expensive. Limit the business concepts down to the top five with them in mind proceed on.

RESEARCH THE IDEA

Although you may have a great idea for soft serve snow cones, Alaska might not be the place to start this business, you will need to do some research. No one can tell if your business will be a complete success or failure. You can dramatically increase your chance of success by careful planning and especially analyzing. What do you need to analyze? And where do you get this information? Let's start right in your home. Head to your computer, google the type of business you want to start in your town. Count how many business listings there are for the type of business you wish to start. Does it seem on every corner there is one? Copy down the names and numbers of the businesses. Do they have a web page? How large are they? Even though there could seem to be a lot of businesses, which you have decided to start, are you going for a specific local economy?

Although most businesses come up in the search, some of them do not do business in that area. Just because this is where they are located does not mean this is where their targeted market exists (or even yours). If there is a certain niche of your business you are focusing on, call the competition, and go to their retail store if possible. Look over their products and their prices they are asking for the goods. Maybe the reason you are starting your own business is local businesses do not service clients properly, or do not have the service you will be offering.

Call your local Chamber of Commerce and ask questions about the population size. Maybe there are enough people in the city to have two used book stores. Determine where your primary target is, (example: dog groomers look at the local Sunday newspaper for the clubs section and search out the dog clubs. Go to one of their meetings and question the members if they are being serviced to their satisfaction).

Research also involves looking into where you will want to set your business up at, the licenses and permits you needs. Your local city or county business license section will have that information. Be nosy. This is your potential bread basket.

There is not a t-shirt shop in my town, there is one in the neighboring town 10 minutes away. Our town is growing, and a lot of people are going to the next town to get their shirts. We have a youth soccer league, which buys uniforms for about 300 kids every year. There are at least 60 businesses in the area, and both school districts buy athletic clothes with their logo on them. I talked with the chamber of commerce, they have programs to help with the business side, as well as networking opportunities to meet potential customers.

The city says I will need a business license. I do not need any special training or stated licenses. I will need to get a resale permit from the state. There are some empty buildings downtown. I called the owners and found out the rent is reasonable. I found a place that sells the equipment on monthly terms so I don't have to have a lot of money up front.

When to Start

Assessing current position

Remember this is **not** an overnight get rich quick scheme - you will need some money to start and keep your business running. Even if your business pays for itself, you still have a house payment (or rent), car payment, credit card payments etc... Compile your bills and the assets which you will be using to start your business and determine if you will need to start part-time, just after work and Saturdays, or whenever you can find the time. Try to stay out of debt going into business. Although the thought of just getting a business loan and having all the finances to start up is nice, if your business does fail, or go on hard times, it is easier to have a loss for the year out of your own savings, instead of having a loan payment to make, and no way of paying for it. Keep in mind some of the hidden advantages for working for someone else, they pay half your taxes, they could have matching funds for your 401K, they could pay for medical insurance, sick days, paid vacation days, and so forth.

Establishing Business Credit

Before giving your boss the goodbye notice, or taking less hours to start your business, utilize your personal credit (and the stability of your job) to get a jump start on your business credit. Lending institutions do not like to risk their money, and while you are bringing home that set paycheck, they are more likely to give a line of credit, than after you have quit and do not have any income to verify. Lending institutions usually ask for two years of self-employment tax returns, to see if they will offer a line of business credit, business loans, or business credit cards. One simple fact about most businesses is that they do not have an actual return on investment (gain) in the first few years. This is why using your good personal credit, and stable job to seek business credit is useful.

Scheduling In Time

Time management skills are a must when operating your own business. Look at the following worksheet. This will be used to view a realistic idea of how much time you really have for starting your business. First off, schedule eight hours for sleep. I know a lot of you will say you never have slept eight hours in your life and you can operate with less, I will tell you now - **you need your sleep.** Research has stated over and over the positive impact of having the sleep your body needs to regenerate itself for your overall health. While other research shows the drastic impact not having enough sleep has on your physical health, your mental health, and really your entire life. Next block out the hours you will still be working for another (if you are). Include these times as well: commuting, getting ready, staying late, etc. Now your family, they need your time too. After that recreation, your brain must have a little play.

I have few thousand dollars saved up, I can use it to get started. Of course I won't have a paycheck for a little while. So we will have to budget our money very well. My wife's income will help us pay the bills in the beginning. Being as my credit is pretty good, I could get a credit card to buy materials with and pay if off when I get paid by the customer. I talked with some suppliers and they have terms I can get with them. I should be able to get net 30 days, which means I can pay for my supplies like t-shirts 30 days after I order them. That way I can get the order finished, deliver it to the customer and get paid. Then I can pay the suppliers.

I am going to do this business fulltime. I will work at the business from 8 am until 5 or 6 pm. I know I will have to put in extra time sometimes in order to make the business grow. I will have some time after the kids go to bed to do work if I need to.

TIME MANAGEMENT WORKSHEET

12:00 AM - _____

1:00 AM - _____

2:00 AM - _____

3:00 AM - _____

4:00 AM - _____

5:00 AM - _____

6:00 AM - _____

7:00 AM - _____

8:00 AM - _____

9:00 AM - _____

10:00 AM - _____

12:00 PM - _____

1:00 PM - _____

2:00 PM - _____

3:00 PM - _____

4:00 PM - _____

5:00 PM - _____

6:00 PM - _____

7:00 PM - _____

8:00 PM - _____

9:00 PM - _____

10:00 PM - _____

11:00 PM - _____

12:00 AM- _____

Now look at the time that is left over after all the necessary hours have been used up. This is the actual time you have to put forth for operating your business. This could be the time that you notice you would much rather work for another person and put in the hours there, as opposed to the increased hours I guarantee your new business will be taking up. Do not fall into the myth that operating your own business will somehow free up time for your family, recreations, or other lofty ideas, in the beginning. There are a lot of hours dedicated to paperwork, managerial functions, accounting functions, which will be added onto producing the product or providing the services your business will be dealing with.

Now that you have your idea, researched the idea, looked over financing options, and checked out time constraints, it's time to plan your business.

WRITING THE BUSINESS PLAN

Many people question whether or not they really need a business plan. Here's a hint . . . **YOU NEED A BUSINESS PLAN!** It would be reckless to travel across the country or into another country without planning the way, and having a map. Think of the business plan as your map for success. Sure some people blindly get there, but do you really want to take that chance? Consider how many businesses fail within the first five years, then add on top of that not having a plan of getting to your goal of success. Without a business plan you are heading down the road to failure. A business plan cannot be written in one evening. After your research is gathered up, it will be used to map out your business road to succeed. It does not matter if your business is just part-time and/or very small. Every business should have a business plan.

One myth about business plans is if the market changes then the plan will not be any good. Business plans are not set in stone. You will need to frequently come back to the plan in the first year and revise it. Revising the plan does not mean it is a step backwards. Sometimes ideas on paper seem like they will flow without problems, but in the real world stuff happens. Another reason to have a business plan is for when you are seeking financing from an institution, they will require to see your business plan. Even if you are asking family, friends, or colleagues for the necessary funds, a business plan will help you convey to them you are serious about this new venture.

This is a vital step in the success of your new business. The better the plan the better the chances of success you will have. You should gather as much information and data as possible. Remember you are the expert of your business. No one will put forth the effort and accuracy as you will. The success of your new business depends on the work you put into it.

There is a multitude of different forms, which are free, to help you construct a good business plan. There are several computer programs available as well as companies who specialized in business plans. You can even ask for a business plan which has already been completed, and use that as a guideline for your plan. Copying another company's plan is the worst possible mistake. That company will not have the same back ground experience, interests, hobbies, and goals as yours. In a simple business plan there are four sections: Executive Summary, Mission Statement, The Business Information and Operations.

Executive Summary:

Name the owners and the form of business it will be (sole proprietorship, partnership, limited liability company, incorporated, etc.). Name the person who will take primary responsibility for managing the business. Give a summary of the business and its goals. List the experience and skills each person brings to the business. Declare the amount of financing and where it will derive from. State how and when the funds will be repaid.

Mission Statement:

A single short paragraph will do for this section. Comprise your guiding principles, purpose for being in business and the unique selling position which you believe will lead to success.

The Business Information:

Describe in detail a description of the business. Describe the background and expertise of owners. Explain the proposed location and benefits of that location. List the product(s) and/or service(s) which your business will supply. What form of ownership with the company have. What relationships will you have with existing businesses and how that will benefit your business? What kind of strategic alliances with professionals will you have? Describe your long-term and short-term goals for the business including your steps and a time line for achieving them.

Operations:

List who will manage the business and the reason(s) why. List the insurance needed, the lease/rent and your suppliers. If you will be hiring employees discuss the staffing needs and the policy for hiring personnel (design a personnel policy pamphlet and have it looked over by a professional). List and describe the equipment needed to operate the business. Discuss how the product(s) will be produced or the service(s) will be provided. Address your customer service, the credit and collection policies (will most accounts be net 30 days?). Examine and state your record keeping methods, and who will keep the records (another agency or will they be in-house). Remember this is just a suggested outline of a business plan and not in the least bit complete.

Here is a list of items which need to be considered in developing and writing a business plan: **description of product and/or service, goals and objectives, proposed or existing business description, personal capabilities and experience, location of the business, financing, accounting procedures, estimated cost of initial start-up, taxes, payroll, market strategy, legal needs, reporting to governmental agencies, insurance, sales and market analysis, your competitive advantages, and a management plan.**

Wow, this is a lot of research. I really just want to start making shirts, but the bank says I need this business plan so they can understand what my business does and how it operates. I went to office depot and found a computer program that helps with writing a business plan. It asks me several questions, I enter the data I discovered in the research and it generates a nice business plan.

This took some time to find all the data, but along the journey I learned a lot about how I am going to run my business. After completing the business plan, I'm glad I did it. It really did help me in more ways than just giving me the paper the bank wanted.

FINANCES

A large part of the business you are thinking about will have to do with the finances it could take to start-up. Start-up costs can range from as little as $50 and go up. There really is not a cap on the amount to start-up a business can be. The first part of looking into finances is putting together a cost-of-living-budget. The following worksheet will help you with this.

COST OF LIVING WORKSHEET

*This list is not all inclusive, add or delete where you need to.

Regular monthly payments/rent or mortgage:	
Car loans:	
Gas:	
Car insurance:	
Personal loans (credit cards, student loans):	
Home improvement loans (second mortgage):	
A health plan:	
Life insurance premiums:	
Miscellaneous:	
Telephone:	
Gas and electricity:	
Water and garbage:	
Other household repairs and expenses:	
Food:	

Clothing:	
Dry cleaners:	
Doctor and dentist (co-pays):	
Gifts and contributions:	
Travel expenses (vacations):	
Newspapers/ magazines/ books:	
Federal/state taxes; property tax; and other taxes:	
Sub-Total	
Income	
Total (subtract sub-total from income)	

You will need to organize what your household is actually costing to operate. Add them all together and you will have an amount of what you normally spend during the month. This amount will determine if you are going to start your business full-time, part-time, or after your regular nine-to-five job for the time being. This amount will also tell you what you will need to bring into the household to be a success. There are certainly some areas that can be cut back on, but this is a realistic amount of what you have been used to having.

Now look at your business plan. Estimate what it will take to keep the business open, and to put money back into the business. This is something that need not be overlooked. You will need to put back money to grow. Some of this money will be for savings to buy better or bigger equipment, or supplies, advertising and other expenses that could come up only now and then. Like an advertising blitz in the first of the year for a good kick off - you will need to have that money in the bank. Be very realistic about what you can and cannot do without. Discuss this with not only your business partners but all persons who will be effected by your decisions.

Take a look into financing. Many people do not have the cash on hand to start a new business. Financing options allow you to get the cash needed to start-up the business and keep it going until the business begins to become self-supportive. Most small businesses are Personally Financed: personal assets; savings, selling off a luxury (an extra car, RV, boat); borrowing against an insurance plan; second mortgage; family members; personal loans and secure loans using some type of collateral.

Debt Financing is borrowing money that is to be repaid, at an interest rate: bank lines of credit, commercial loans, equipment leasing, and letters of credit from banks and credit unions. The Small Business Administration has money (loans) set aside for start-up cost on approved businesses (YOU WILL NEED A BUSINESS PLAN

TO SHOW THEM). When estimating the operating cost of your business (if you are using this type of funding) make sure your account for the interest or end purchase price on leased equipment.

The last type of financing which needs to be mentioned even though it is used minimally with small business is Equity financing. Equity financing means to exchange money for ownership or part ownership of the business. Depending on the type of organization you are dealing with this could include: venture capital, selling owner shares in the form of stocks, franchising and private investors. Make sure if this is the way you are financing your business, you account for the percentage as well as fees and possibly interest rates which will need to be paid before your personal check is written.

Credit History

When any type of lender looks at you for loans or investment, they check out the four C's: Credit History, Collateral, Cash Flow and Character. Lenders will review your other business credit history as well as your personal history (this is where that late credit card payment will have to be explained). Before you get any surprises from lending institutions, get a copy of your own credit history and look it over. If there are any discrepancies fight them. Make sure all persons who will be taking on part of the financial risk have their credit reports checked too. There are several ways to check your credit, one really good free website is creditkarma.com

Collateral

If for some reason your business closes, what do you own which could be sold to cover the bills. If one of your partners takes all the money out of the bank and leaves for Mexico, you will be left alone holding the bag of bills. Collateral is using an item (car, boat) to secure the loan. If you do not repay the loan, the institution takes the item (car, boat) to pay the loan off. Be cautious. Even if you have placed something for collateral on the loan, after the item is sold, if it does not cover what you owned, you still will be required to make up the difference.

Cash Flow

Cash Flow is one of the most important factors in securing short-term financing. This consists of money that is coming in (sales) and money going out (expenses) of the business on a daily basis. Lenders will weigh if the business can generate enough money to pay its bills and repay the loans on time. Some businesses deal in the net 30 category. Once the bill is created, they have 30 days in which to pay it. So your expenses could add up before the money begins to flow in.

The lender will want to know what type of accounts receivable you are working off of: payment on receipt of goods; payment on receipt of the bill, net 30, net 60 or so forth. Dealing with governmental agencies as customers sometimes will be very frustrating; they work on you get paid when the check arrives. Know who your potential customers are. Make sure if you are going to be conducting business with clients who do not pay on receipt of goods/bill, that their history of payment is worked into your business plan.

Finally Character

This does count in the business world. The lender will be looking for referrals from other professionals, past relationships with them and/or other institutions, or successful prior business experience. Be prepared to provide the business plan, your personal financial statement (this consists of what you have - assets; and what you owe - liabilities), estimated start-up costs, projected balance sheets, your projected income taxes, and a description of collateral (if using any and the estimate market value) for securing the loan.

KEEPING RECORDS

After personally being through an IRS audit, I cannot ***stress*** the importance of keeping good records. Record keeping is a **VERY** essential and significant part of a successful business. Even if you enjoy tearing through the office trying to find where you put the receipts for three years ago, **KEEP GOOD RECORDS OF EVERYTHING.**

This is where your personality comes into play. If you are not good at writing down your check numbers, amounts, and where you wrote them to in your personal life, do not believe somehow you will change this behavior in your business life. **Get HELP!** There are agencies which will do accounting as well as keeping vital records for you. Even if you have to hire someone to come in and work, it is better in the long run. Organized business records are yet another step for help in reaching the successful business goal. What you will keep records on, is determined by your type of business. Remember income taxes come once a year, but you could end up paying for a lifetime on a few minor mistakes. The IRS does have the authority to take your assets and sell them to pay off your taxes.

Keeping an organized account, of who owes you, who you owe, and when you have paid something is essential. It cannot be stressed enough to keep good, organized records of your business. Many small businesses have gone into the red because records were not kept which could have proven a bill was or was not paid, or a tax was paid. Do not rely on your customers or your suppliers, or even your lender to keep the records for you - this is allowing someone else to make or break your business. There are a lot of other things your mind should be concentrated on, and one of them is not if a company has been paid, or a customer has paid their bill. Financial records are not only the records you will need to keep: leasing agreements (rent on the building), licenses, sellers permit, fire marshal permits, contracts (your partner contract), and other such records.

A good suggestion I received from a local CPA was to spend a little now, to save a lot of heart ache (and possibly money) later. There are accounting kits which can be purchased where you obtain your business checks. These kits have in them the ability while you are writing a check to simultaneously be duplicating that check into a journal ledger. There are also a lot of software programs which can be utilized to help out not only with balancing your check book, but remind you to pay bills, comprise a profit loss statement, post your checks automatically into your journal ledgers, and so forth. There is so much help in programs, software, and gadgets for keeping a grip on your accounting, that there is not excuse to not utilize one of these systems.

So this is something I am not real good at. Actually, I just do not like it. When I was at office depot, I found a computer program called QuickBooks. It made my record keeping so much easier. I did not have to learn how to be a CPA. The program was just like writing a check. I enter the information into the simple forms and the program does all the work. The only real challenge I have now is to actually enter the data. I found over time that when I piled up the receipts and invoices for the month, and tried to enter them all at once, I got frustrated and it took a long time. I even forgot some things. But when I took a few minutes every day to do the bookkeeping, it went so much more smoothly. Doing this really made it easier, and I did not mind it so much. I also had more accurate records.

GETTING STARTED

Now you have the business idea, researched the idea, the time, looked over finances, let's get started. The first thing you need to decide is the organizational structure of your business. Will your new business be a sole-proprietorship, an LLC, a corporation or some other structure? If you will be conducting business under some name (example: Preferred Pets), other than your own (example: Jane Smith's pampered pets) you have to have get a fictitious business name. You can use your own name and not have a fictitious business name, but most do not. If the name you have chosen is already in use, do not just add an A or The, but change it. You really do not want to be linked to another business with your name. You could think because the other business has such a great reputation, it would be an asset. **Do not do it**. Reputation can diminish overnight. Plus, legally your name should not be so close with another.

Once you have found your name is not in use, or you have changed your name, fill out a simple form and pay the fee for your new business name at the county office. Different states will operate in different ways, so you may get several copies back or some other form of paper designating your new fictitious business name. One copy is for opening your business bank account. Another can be used to place an announcement in a publication (necessary by law in some states), and the other is for your own records.

Your state's Board of Equalization will be your next stop, to apply for a resale license. This is a necessary license to purchase products wholesale, and also for the State to keep track and collect the sales taxes you will be collecting from your clients.

You will need to find out from your local city hall, or county office if a business license is necessary for your establishment. Even if you will be operating a home-based business, you will still have to go to these places. Make sure if you are conducting business from your home that you have the rules and regulation, and there are rules and regulations for having a home-based business in quite a lot of areas.

*I decided to start very simple, as a sole-proprietorship. I could have used my name like **Doug's T-shirt Factory**, but I chose to call the company **Special T's**. Because I did not use my name, I had to get a fictitious business name from the county. That was not hard, a few dollars and filing at the court house and it was done. I rented a building downtown, got a phone line and ordered the equipment.*

A bonus I found out later was the company I ordered the equipment from, actually did training for free. They delivered the equipment and a person came the next day, set up the equipment and spent the next two days training me on how to use it.

Hidden Licenses and Fees

In some industries, there are associations which require you to pay fees, go through a seminar/schooling, or obtain a certain certification (example: satellite installer's association fee). Some states also require extra licensing for certain businesses (example: barber license). So do the research and find out. It is not advantageous to operate outside the law.

Taxes

One item overlooked by first time business owners are the higher taxes self-employed people pay, and the issue of sales tax. These two issues can get you in serious trouble if not realized and understood. All tax issues need to be discussed with your CPA and/or with the IRS.

Owning your own business means no longer will another pay half of your taxes for you. Self-employment taxes are approximately 30%, as opposed to the 15% you pay when working for another (your employer pays the other 15%). The first time filling out your Schedule C might be a real eye opener. You need to start thinking and calculating the extra taxes which will be owed to the government. Sure there are write offs such as business expenditures, but do not think that you have gone into business to save on your taxes, because that is no reason to start a business, and you will not be saving.

Sales tax is a very different story. As a business owner you will collect sales taxes from your clients for the products and/or services you provide. Sales tax is dependent on the place you are doing business and where the transaction takes place at. It usually is added on top of the price, but some people include their taxes in their products. Remember, this is the State's money and should be placed into a separate savings account (if you have trouble with money). This money is **not** part of your business finances and should **not** be used for anything except handing over to the State. Depending on your state the sales tax can be paid quarterly, semi-annually, annually or other. Some states allow you to pick which you want, but ask before assuming that it is just paid on an annual basis.

MARKETING

Billions of dollars are spent every year on businesses marketing their products to their customers. Be very careful in this venture. You will need to market your business, but make sure you do your research. Radio ads, newspaper ads, business cards, promotional products, cost and some a lot more than the others. Be very frugal about how much and where you do your advertising. Numerous low cost and free ways of marketing are overlooked for the pricey corporate way. You do not have Pepsi-Colas cash flow, so do not think you can get a 30 second ad during the super bowl. Be reasonable and budget your advertising account. You should be able to have measurable returns on all your advertising.

Free advertising

Yes, there are ways to market your business for free. One is the local newspapers. Most newspapers contain business sections. Some of them will allow you to write your own little ad about your new business. Just as a new business is news, so is all the promotions, workshops, new products/services, so write up little blurbs and send them in. A few minutes on the computer, a stamp, and an envelope can create some free advertising.

Another free way to advertise is word of mouth. Get your friends, relatives to just say something about the new business your opening. You never know when this could turn into a new account. You are also a free way to advertise. You should have about a 30 second commercial you have memorized where you can tell someone how your business provides a product or service. Memorize it, how many times have you left a conversation remembering you wanted to say something and did not. If you memorize this, it will soon come out as natural as your name.

> *Getting the word out about my business was a challenge for me. I really did not know where to start. I discovered the local paper printed free articles about new businesses and updates on businesses. So I sent them articles telling about my business, which the paper printed for free. Any time I had a promotion, a new product etc., I would send the paper an article, which they printed in the business section for free.*

Business Cards

A very inexpensive way to advertise is your business card. Business cards should be eye catching and professionally done. There is nothing that says your business is low budget (which gets the customer thinking low quality) more than a business card that has been produced by a computer program and you can still see the ridges where it had been perforated at. Professionalism is a must, even on a budget.

> *I stumbled across a company on the internet called Vista Print. They print business cards and other items at great prices. I had a very nice business card created, which had my contact information and explained exactly what my business does. The cards looked great. I always carried them with me and told*

everyone I talked to about my business. I never left a conversation without giving them a business card.

Promotional Products

Look inside your purse or in your car. How many pens do you have that are from businesses with their names on them? How many magnets on your refrigerator are sporting business logos? Businesses purchase pens as well as other items to have their name in front of their clients, and possibly passed on to potential clients. These items are given out free, yes free. The concept behind promotional products is to have your business name out there as much as possible. Be cautious about purchasing promotional products which might offend someone (example: an ash tray from a funeral chapel, with "ashes to ashes" as their motto). For almost all businesses the following ten top promotional products will be fine: Pens, T-shirts, Mugs, Calendars, Hats, Magnets, Stress Balls, Key chains, Water bottles and Letter openers.

Industry Associations

All trades have some industry association which can usually be found online. These associations can be an invaluable resources to industry trends, information, sources, suppliers, and can even generate clients. Even if you do not become a member of the association do book mark the site and visit it often for updated free information.

Put yourself on the mailing lists of your industry associations even if you do not join. They should still inform you of upcoming conventions, workshops and seminars. They do this to have you see them as an invaluable resource and try prompting you to join. Also make it a habit to add your business address to every mailing list which had something to do with your industry. It's amazing what other companies send for free (promotional products, tickets, free subscriptions, samples, etc.)

Along with the associations, most industries have conventions of some sort which can be attended. Conventions, workshops, and seminars can connect you with otherwise unknown information and resources inside your industry. Continual education should be every entrepreneur's motto.

After talking to suppliers and others in the industry, I found there was a screen printers association and I could join for free. This association put on conferences and seminars over the year. They sent me information and invitations to these conferences and seminars. I attended as many and as often as I could. Also on their website I found lots of great information, which over time allowed me to gain knowledge in the industry. Over the next couple of years I was able to become a master screen printer. Because of the knowledge and help I received, I got to the point where I found myself helping others in the industry improve their skills.

Networking

Networking is many times not used (or known about) for first time business owners. Most chamber of commerce have some type of networking meetings to attend. These social events can generate new clients and give you a feel for how other businesses are doing in your local area. Become a member and put forth time to network. It is time well invested.

Lead Groups fall under networking also. Lead groups are people (usually business owners) belonging to a club to give leads to other members of the group. Some leads are referrals, others are just utilizing your business. Usually there is a fee for joining this group, and at each meeting the ticket into the meeting is one or more leads. Usually only one business in each area will be allowed to join (example: one doctor, one lawyer, one salon). Be careful of these groups. Even though in large metropolitan area they are invaluable to some businesses, in other areas you can utilize your time better with joining the chambers (there is more networking opportunities, especially if the Lead Group is small). You will need to weigh the benefit of the group compared to how much time at meetings and dues you have to pay. Marketing is all about the return on your investment.

PROFESSIONALISM

Whether your business will be cleaning toilets or negotiating million dollar off-shore business deals, you need to remember to be professional in every manner of your business. Any materials coming from your business must have a professional quality to them, from your business cards to the memos to clients who have forgotten to pay their bills. Do not print up some quick flyers on the computer that look like your toddler did the layouts for. Analyze all your marketing mediums and ask yourself if you saw that item, would you want to do business with them?

Talk professional. This is not meant to look up new un-circulated words and use them as your everyday vocabulary. Do brush up on your English and definitely leave swearing out, that is what people who have very poor vocabulary use. Try to educate your clients on the jargon of your industry and also on your business. Talk for success.

Dress professionally. I laugh when I hear the commercial "image is nothing, obey your thirst", you probably know the one too. If image was really nothing why did that soda company spend millions on telling you so? Image does matter. Your product could be the next paper clip but if you do not properly dress the product, and yourself, someone will most likely take your idea and make millions. I do not mean go buy an Armani suit to sell toilet cleaners (there are some salespeople who do), but also do not slip on hole-filled sweats, a greased t-shirt and think your product will shine. Take a good look in the mirror, and analyze, be critical, your financial stability could very well depend on it.

There is a professional way to see your products and services as well. Everything leaving your business has your name on it, and you want the best image possible. Do not allow shabby products to leave your warehouse. It is much easier to talk with a client about the possible lateness of delivery than having a client tell her friends about your lousy work. Research has shown when a client is dissatisfied she tells eight of her friends. Just imagine if those eight friends told another eight friends, and then so on and so on. I think you get the idea. Bad word of mouth is poison for your business.

Everywhere I went, I was my own best commercial. I found myself sitting in restaurants eating dinner with my family, when the manager came by, I would ask him where he got his shirts printed. This started a conversation which ended in me giving him my card and setting a follow up appointment to give him a quote.

My wife actually taught me one of the most valuable lessons in our business, professionalism. Every job we did was completed with total professionalism. The products we did were the best we could produce, folded and packaged very neatly. Anything our logo went on, was the best it could be, very clean and professional. I learned to ensure things were spelled correctly and looked good. (Well this actually took some time and lots of reminding from my wife, But I did learn the extreme value of it.)

OWNER'S CHECKLIST

This is just a sample of a checklist to get you thinking about what you will need to start this road to success. The list is in no particular order, you will determine what needs to be done first. This list is not all inclusive. Its purpose is to kick start your thinking about what needs to be done in order to start your new business.

Research work

- ❖ Assess your strengths and weaknesses and your partner(s)
- ❖ Organize business and personal goals
- ❖ Identify financial risks
- ❖ Determine start-up costs
- ❖ Assess your financial resources
- ❖ Decide on the business location
- ❖ Do customer research
- ❖ Identify your competitors

Business transactions

- ❖ Search out a compatible lawyer
- ❖ Choose an entity (Sole-proprietorship, partnership, LLC or corporation)
- ❖ Prepare a Business Plan
- ❖ Select a banker
- ❖ Select an accountant
- ❖ Secure financing
- ❖ Obtain business insurance
- ❖ Establish a line of credit

Before Opening the Doors

- ❖ Get business cards
- ❖ Obtain a lease
- ❖ Send off for federal and state tax forms
- ❖ Obtain licensing or permit
- ❖ Review local building codes
- ❖ Get promotional products
- ❖ Purchase/find furniture and equipment
- ❖ Get a tax ID number
- ❖ Get an employer ID number
- ❖ Join a professional organization
- ❖ Line up suppliers
- ❖ Propose a start date
- ❖ **Tell EVERYONE about your new venture**

SUMMING IT UP

This book has provided enough information to begin the road of success. Remember Microsoft was not build in a day. You do have the determination and the strength inside of you to obtain your successful business goal. Keep your feet on the earth, but let your mind soar with the eagles. Patience and hard work do pay off, and what is really important about this beginning is the ability to say "*I can do it*." Even first businesses, which close early, will give education about what you can do differently. The only mark of failure is to not try at all!!

Now take the list of resources that have been provided below and find out as much as possible about your business idea. There are lots of free agencies willing to help you succeed, but you must know of them and ask for their help.

HELPFUL RESOURCES

American Marketing Association
www.ama.org

United States Census Bureau
www.census.gov

Better Business Bureau
www.bbb.org

Chamber of Commerce
Google your local chamber of commerce. Services vary among different chambers. Some give advice, support, workshops, seminars, local business news, and other services specifically for small business.

International Revenue Service (IRS)
www.irs.gov

Occupational Safety & Health Administration (OSHA)
www.osha.com

Small Business Administration (SBA)
www.sba.gov
Go Daddy
www.godaddy.com

Vista Print
www.vistaprint.com

Legal Zoom
www.legalzoom.com

Quick Books
www.intuit.com

www.ingramcontent.com/pod-product-compliance
Lightning Source LLC
Chambersburg PA
CBHW032019190326
41520CB00007B/536